Worship HYMNS FOR ORGAN

Volume III

ARRANGED BY CAROLYN HAMLIN

TABLE OF CONTENTS

Fred Bock Music Company

EXCLUSIVELY DISTRIBUTED BY

HAL•LEONARD

for Betty Bennett
Music faculty, Gardner-Webb University

PRAISE TO THE LORD, THE ALMIGHTY

Sw. Flutes 8', 4', 2', Octave 4'
Gt. Principals 8', 4', 2', Flutes 8', 4', 2', Mixture IV, Sw. to Gt.
Ch. Festival Trumpet 8'
Ped. Diapason 16', Octave 8', 4', Bourdon 16', Gedeckt 8', Gt. to Ped.

Stralsund Gesangbuch
Arranged by CAROLYN HAMLIN (ASCAP)

With joyous praise (♩. = 76)

Sw. Solo Reed 8', Flute 4'
Gt. Diapason 8', Flutes 8', 4'
Ped. Bourdon 16', Gedeckt 8'

Sw.
Opening registration
Gt.
slight rit.
Sw. Reeds 16', 8', 4'
Gt. Diapason 8', Octave 4', 2' Super Octave
Ch. Flutes 8', 4', 2'
Ped. Bourdon 16', Flutes 8', 4', Gt. to Ped.
a little slower
Gt.
Sw.
slight rit.
a tempo
Gt.
Sw.
slight rit.

52
Gt. Add Ch. to Gt.
Gt.
a tempo
Gt. Add Mixture IV
Ped. Add Diapason 16 '
57
61
rit.
Full organ, no reeds
Grandioso
65

69
72
75
Full organ with reeds
much slower
78
molto rit.

for Tina Boyd Wagoner

LAND OF REST

With "Going Home" ("Largo" from Antonin Dvorak's *From the New World*, op. 95)

Sw. Bourdon 8', Oboe 8'
Gt. Harmonic Flute 8', Flute 4'
Ch. Viole 8', Viole Celeste
Ped. Lieblich Gedeckt 16', Flute 8'

American Folk Hymns
Arranged by CAROLYN HAMLIN (ASCAP)

With much expression (♩ = 112)

12
16
Sw.
Gt.
19
Ch.
23

27
Ch.
slight rit.
31
Gt.
a tempo
slight rit.
Sw. String 8', String Celeste
Gt. Flutes 8', 4', Gamba 8', Gamba Celeste
Ch. Flute 8', Viole, Viole Celeste, Sw. to Ch.
35
"Going Home" (Folk Hymn/Dvorak)
Ch.
a tempo
slight rit.
39
a tempo

Sw. String 8', String Celeste, Vox Humana, Trem.
Gt. Flute 8', Gamba 8', Gamba Celeste, Sw. to Gt., Ch. to Gt., Trem.
Ch. Flute 8', Flute Celeste, Viole, Viole Celeste, Sw. to Ch., Trem.
Ped. Bourdon 16', Gedeckt 8'

*Sw. Solo Trumpet 8'
Gt. Diapason 8', Flutes 8', 4', 2', Octave 4'
Ch. Gedeckt 8', Principal 4'
Ped. Bourdon 16', Flute 8', Ch. to Ped.

for Joy Collins,
a humble servant of the Lord Jesus Christ,
whose life and keyboard artistry reflect His truth and beauty

GIVE ME JESUS

Sw. Viola, Viola Celeste
Gt. Waldhorn 8'
Ch. Salicional, Salicional Celeste, Sw. to Ch.
Ped. Bourdon 16', Sw. to Ped.

Traditional Spiritual
Arranged by CAROLYN HAMLIN (ASCAP)

15
Sw.
20
Gt.
25
Ch.
29

Sw. Flutes 8', 4'
Gt. Diapason 8', Flutes 4', 2', Sw. to Gt., Ch.. to Gt.
Ch. Flutes 8', 4', Sw. to Ch.
Ped. Bourdon 16', Flute 8', Ch. to Ped.

Gt. Add Octave 4', Super Octave 2'
Ped. Add Diapason 16'
55
Gt.
61
rit.
a tempo
Sw. Solo Trumpet 8'
Gt. Diapason 8', Octave 4', Flutes 8', 4', 2', Ch. to Gt.
Ch. Flutes 8', 4', 2'
Ped. Diapason 16', Octave 8', Principal 4', Gt. to Ped.
66
Sw.
slight rit.
a tempo
Gt.
72

77
Gt.
Add Reed 16'
Sw. Flutes 8', 4', 2', Mix. III
Gt. Principal 8', Octave 4', Super Octave 2', Flutes 4', 2', Mix. IV, Sw. to Gt., Ch. to Gt.
Ch. Flutes 8', 4', 2', Octave 4'
Ped. Diapason 16', Bourdon 16', Octave 8', Flute 8', Mix.
81
Gt.
Sw. Flutes 8', 4'
Gt. Principal 8', Flute 4', Sw. to Gt., Ch. to Gt.
Ch. Flute 4', Sw. to Ch.
Ped. Bourdon 16'
86
slight rit.
Gt.
90
Opening registration
Ch.

for Dr. Ed Dunbar, Chairman,
Division of Music, Bob Jones University

ALL HAIL THE POWER OF JESUS' NAME

Sw. Solo Trumpet 8'
Gt. Principal 8', Flute 4', Octave 4', Piccolo 2', Ch. to Gt., Mix. IV
Ch. Flutes 8', 4'
Ped. Bourdon 16', Diapason 8', Flute 8', Octave 4'

OLIVER HOLDEN
Arranged by CAROLYN HAMLIN (ASCAP)

With majesty ♩ = 106

12
16
20
Gt.
Sw. Flutes 8', 4'
Gt. Diap. 8', Flute 8', Sw. to Gt. 8', Ch. to Gt. 8'
Ch. Flute 8'
Ped. Sw. to Ped. 16', 8'
A little slower
24
Gt.

27
31
Tempo I (♩ = 106)
Gt. Add Octave 4', Super Octave 2', Flute 2'
34
Gt. Add Mix. IV
Ped. Gt. to Ped.
38

*Sw. Flutes 8', 4', 2', Octave 4', Mix. III, Reeds 16', 8', 4'
Gt. Principal 8', Octave 4', Flutes 8', 4', Super Octave 2', Mix. IV, Tromba 8', Sw. to Gt. 8', Ch to Gt. 8'
Ch. Flutes 8', 4', 2', Mix. III
Ped. Diapasons 16', 8', 4', Mix. IV, Reeds 16', Gt. to Ped.

Broader

55
58
Full organ with reeds
Broader
slight rit.
62
slight rit.
a tempo
66

for Phill Burnett

SIMPLE GIFTS

Sw. Chiffy Flute 8'
Gt. Flutes 8', 4'
Ch. Krumhorn 8'
Ped. Flute 16'

Traditional Shaker Melody
Arranged by CAROLYN HAMLIN (ASCAP)

13
17
Gt.
Ch.
21
Sw.
Sw. String 8', String Celeste, Vox Humana
Gt. Flute 8', Gamba 8', Sw. to Gt., Ch. to Gt.
Ch. String 8', String Celeste
Ped. Soft Flute 16'
25
Gt.
Sw.

28
32
36
Gt.
Sw.
40

Sw. Trompette 8'
Gt. Diapason 8', Octave 4', Flute 4', Principal 2', Ch. to Gt.
Ch. Flutes 8', 4'
Ped. Bourdon 16'
44
Gt.
Gt.
48
Sw.
52
Sw. Add Reed 4'
Gt. Add Mix. IV
Ch. Add Flute 2', Mix. III
Ped. Add Diapason 16', Reed 16'
56
Gt.

61
Sw.
65
Opening registration
Sw.
Sw. Flute 4'
Ch. String 8', String Celeste
Ped. Soft Flute 16'
a little slower
69
Sw.
slight rit.
Ch.
73
poco a poco rit. to end

for Charlie Jones

LO! HOW A ROSE E'ER BLOOMING

Sw. Oboe
Gt. Harmonic Flute 8', Ch. to Gt.
Ch. Flute 8', Flute Celeste
Ped. Soft Flute 16'

Geistliche Kirchengesäng
Arranged by CAROLYN HAMLIN (ASCAP)

In hushed reverence (𝅗𝅥 = 38)

12
15
Gt.
19
Sw.
23
Gt.

Sw. String 8', String Celeste, Vox Humana
Gt. Gamba 8', Sw. to Gt., Ch. to Gt.
Ch. String 8', String Celeste
Ped. Bourdon 16', Ch. to Ped.

Sw. Soft Reed (Midi French Horn)
Gt. Diapason 8', Flutes 8', 4', Ch. to Gt.
Ch. Flutes 8', 4'
Ped. Bourdon 16', Flute 8'

54
58
Gt.
Sw.
61
slowing to end
Sw. String 8', String Celeste
Gt. Flute Celeste 8', Sw. to Gt.
Ped. Lieblich Gedeckt 16'
65
Gt.
molto rit.